The Elem:ents (Nam:loz)

The Elem:ents (Nam:loz)

by

Erín Mou:re

Published in Canada in 2019 and the USA in 2019
by House of Anansi Press Inc.
www.houseofanansi.com

House of Anansi Press is committed to protecting our natural environment. As part of our efforts, the interior of this book is printed on paper made from second-growth forests and is acid-free.

23 22 21 20 19 1 2 3 4 5

Library and Archives Canada Cataloguing in Publication

Moué, Erin, 1955–, author
The elements / Erín Moure.
Poems.
Issued in print and electronic formats.
ISBN 978-1-4870-0372-2 (softcover).—ISBN 978-1-4870-0373-9 (hardcover).—ISBN 978-1-4870-0374-6 (PDF)

I. Title.

PS8576.O96E44 2019 C811'.54 C2018-904759-3
C2018-904760-7

Library of Congress Control Number: 2018961234

Cover image: "Bonitas" (The Good), August Schreitmüller sculpture, raised 1908/1910 on Dresden City Hall, photo by Richard Peter, Autumn 1945. © SLUB Dresden / Deutsche Fotothek / Richard Peter sen.

Bonitas or Good is also Kindness, Tenderness. These are the elements. The gestures. In us, they are the what-it-is.

Canada Council for the Arts Conseil des Arts du Canada

We acknowledge for their financial support of our publishing program the Canada Council for the Arts, the Ontario Arts Council, and the Government of Canada.

Something does interfere.
Art returns.

Paul Celan
The Meridian, 1960

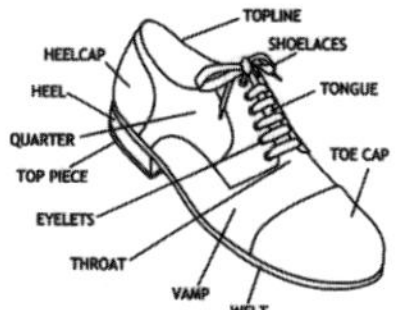

Pop, Dad, Paw, Papy, Papai:
William Benito Moure
December 20, 1925 Ottawa—August 21, 2013 Edmonton
For my brothers, my nieces and nephews, my great-nieces and great-nephew: we are remember.

Restlessness of the Interior

Each behaviour and each form of human living is never prescribed by a particular biological function, nor assigned by any necessity; even though habitual, repeated and socially obligatory, it always retains the character of a possibility. In other words, in every behaviour and form, living itself is always put into play. This is why, insofar as humans are beings of power, who can act or not act, succeed or fail, lose or find ourselves, we are the only beings for whom happiness is always implied in living, the only beings whose life is irremediably and achingly linked to happiness. From the start, this constitutes our form-of-life as political life.

Giorgio Agamben, *Moyens sans fins*, tr. EM

Introjection

IN FACT, de la Cuesta tried to retreat from the French of Napoleon on the plains at Rioseco to salvage his own Castilian army—& so ordered the 4th div. of Blake's Galicians as fodder to the fray, including Pascual Moure, to cover his retreat and its reception, where these are separate AND where they coincide, in translation or otherwheres, necessarily involves the body. Following developments in feminist and performance critical theory since the 1970s and 1980s, we now recognize more freely the polyvalent nature of bodies and social demarcations of gendering, the existence of cultural markings on "the body," and the impossibility of saying "the body" without immediately problematizing the term. The "infinitely transmissible" of Derrida—which we could call poetry (without staking out an origin), or poetry in translation (without staking out a difference between this and "poetry")—demands this polyvalent body. It demands compositional loop&s that enter the transmission process/es differentially, transversally, through bodies, yes, but other polyvalent bodies: not the reified bordered bodies that we bring singly to the doctor to report physical pain (which is, yes, a sign that the body we reify exists as such), but bodies each without (one set of) organs. A body is prostheticized as it aestheticizes language and acts of language. Language is also a prosthe&is.

14 July 1808
Medina de Rioseco

THE ASTURIAN division cut off at Zornotza, Blake's retreating Galicians abruptly turned on the pursuing French at Valmaseda to free their comrades. 2 days later, after 2 hours' fury at Güeñes, the Advance of the 4th were overrun, night fell and Blake pulled back to Espinosa de los Monteros, where on the 10th, joined by La Romana's Baltics, his *Devanceiros* of the 4th held centre with 6 guns. Until. Blake's tactic of frenzy and attack in ruins, his "half-famished brigands" scattered pell-mell, abandoning caissons, fleeing in disarray, led then in tatters by Blake up cold Cantabrian passes to evade pursuit. Thousands imprisoned by the French were forced to Russia, not to return till Napoleon's defeat. Removed from command in favour of La Romana, who awaited troops to support the English, Blake rallied his hounded men south to León, Joaquín Blake, descendent of Irish who'd donned Spanish blue to shoot at the English, in Heidegger the difference between essence & existence, thematized as ontological, between Being and being, becomes the central problem of philosophy. That Being abandons being means: Being cloaks itself in the Manifest Being of being. Being itself is essentially what dissimulates in absconding. Metaphysics: the primacy of being, as Being is abandoned. Blake's hideous aporia. His *Devanceiros* of the 4th had lost their guns (say some) or dragged them in frozen ruts alongside the miserable foot: "Oh Lord open now our lips that they may give <<forth our praise."

31 October - 10 November 1808
Zornotza (Pancorbo), Güeñes, Espinosa de los Monteros

HUNDREDS DROPPED by the roadside on the way to Coruña; broken carts, mules and horses, women and children fell in the mountain snows. Strongboxes of English coin, useless for any purchase, were flung on the death of their beasts into the *caborcos.* Fatigue, depression of mind, and want of shoes broke the march. Without clothes and oppressed by every misery, Moore's retreating English broke down and filled the hospitals. Pus came from their mouths which were but sores; that food was *ausent* no longer mattered for the body had no way to give it entry. Swollen rains burst the carcasses of men and beasts, fouling the air and convulsing stomachs. In the *ti en einai,* Aristotle struggles to articulate as one what has been divided: Being is that which *was being.* All that is identified, as such, already has a past; each time, Being must be presupposed by and supposed in language. Politics and ontology need each other to emerge; Being is chronogenetic. Pain felt by the body is thus a task for history. Fructose is obtained by plants at the water's surface. When existential Being and articulated Being, *zoe* and *bios,* are entirely dissociated as they are today, the historic task of their articulation is unachievable in a single body. Once caught up, La Romana's men plunged into this wine-stupored and heterogeneous mass of marauders and muleteers, disgusted at English perfidy. This body, this pain. Rain and snows. A once-mighty horse of Albion shot by its rider, fallen, its hide culled and wrapped—still wet—round the feet for &hoes.

18 December 1808 - 3 January 1809
Retreat to Corunna

FOR ARISTOTLE, being is constitutively something that "is said" and "signifies." Animal is thus the predicate of Man. The term "predication" is pertinent: every Being wears the shadow of language. Its sediment is substance. Even the unsayable is linguistic, uniquely human for its accusation is one no animal can conceive. The accusative is object of a transitive verb. Hypostasis is pure existence prior to Attribute. Between A Chaira and Lugo, the French came down like thunder, but met resistance and fled into the walls of the Roman city, leading to the ludicrous situation of the invaders defending from inside the polis. Being has no sense except in relation to the other. The person or *prosopon* is both mask and face. In this argument the Trinity is a salvatory gesture. With villagers hoisting hoes and hunting carbines, La Romana's Galicians, now detached from Moore, no more a rearguard, carried out the attacks they could on the arms stores and supply lines of the French. What is at stake is nothing less than the ontological space between Being and being that, to Heidegger, defines Western metaphysics. In 1943, H. wrote that Being can certainly exist without being, but never may being exist without Being. The 5th ed., 1949, after the catastrophe, corrects "certainly" to "never." In 1809, Galicia and Asturias combined could not furnish 300 horses. 6 days later, at A Chaira, Moore's troops were ordered to slip away from the French without fighting, first shooting 500 foundered horses and blowing up their own artillery and food.

6 - 14 January 1809
Lugo

If the poem itself refuses to perform in English

DEFEATED AND shoeless, clothes in shreds or simply missing, Moore's sails long vanished over Biscay, the Galicians continued to emerge from the southern oaks and gorse west of Ribadavia to wreak havoc on the invaders, those *républicains de France* whose armaments dwarfed theirs. Uniformless for three years after the defeats by Napoleon: Rioseco, Zornotza, Güeñes, Espinosa (every town down the king's road from Bilbao) and the retreat in frozen rags through the mountains ("exhausted, destitute, and ravaged by fever; every house we entered was full of those miserable beings, quite destitute of clothing and food") behind Moore's fleeing English—who turned to fight the French at Elviña in Coruña to save not even an idea of Spain but themselves—, few soldiers could be distinguished from locals. Thus the Peninsular origin of guerrilla warfare, north of the Miño: curiously vestimentary. As in the vocabulary of ancient medicine, crisis designated the failing point when the illness had unrelentingly taken hold. Philosophy is one way to measure this, becoming human or destituted. To every name, an existence in p&rticular, unliquidated by dialectic. Aristotelian ontology is here directed toward hypostasis. La Romana's Galicians dispersed to the *aldeas*; to hold fast against the French invaders, they had first to round their slack intestines, and find shoes. *Three years later, at A Coruña by ship and packed south by mule, bolts of uniform cloth* arrived at last, and tailors.*

end January 1809
absque vestitu

felted, unfra*yable

ITH SOULT'S troops heading south to Portugal, the *habitans gallaecs* floated boats to the far bank of the Miño and sank their ferries, leaving the fluvius *inguéable,* from the Frankish that remains in the tongue of the Hexagon, enriching Latin, the first substrate. At the French demand to provide food and wine for 20,000 troops daily, the *habitans* of Arbo and Crecente arose under the abbott of Vilar-e-Couto. Bearing forks, hoes and scythes to defend their homes and food, they made for the bridges. At As Achas, ten of La Houssaye's dragoons fell; the next day, the skirmish left 15 dragoons dead and their horses taken, plus 51 made prisoner. On Ash Wednesday, of 16 dragoons three fled and 13 were killed or taken prisoner; over at the Mourentán bridge the *gallaec* resisters, gaunt with hunger and fear, rained down stones and held till the column of French dismounted, wading beneath to take the village and torch it, burning animals and people alike in the corrals and houses. The effect, orphic, returns to a field of exteriority of pure heterogeneity, in which Chronos wants to die, for time is heterogeneous before it is successive; chronology but one way to represent time. In a melée, s/he with the longest blade triumphs. Here the relation between essence and existence, which Aristotle had thought resolved, becomes the central problem of

ontoll*ogy.

13 - 18 February 1809
the Galician Risings

**tolle lege*

The Accidents (Merlín)

That day I went into the trees
—Give me nothing

My scope was interwoven
birds sang their low

cuckoo thing
easily a wave

Small insects rose up into the wave of
Openly

—Ábreme a luzporta!

Swimming in mere air or sheer air
not quite sure

—Could about be
Yet why put such words in a single monstrance?

Open as those trees
Our mermaid is
its long branches trail out to a leaf or vein

My mermaid is
bark's integument so salutory to view

Give me nothing
Give me not this monstrance
The elements

For which I went today in morning
my mouth black
in the lightcup of the trees

SON OF a nun and a demon, Merlín was conceived to lure humans into darkness, but as he grew, decided to do the opposite. It is said he was able to speak with animals, change form, become invisible, and alter the weather and the elements, and he used these skills with care so as not to rile Nature. He knew of the laws that rule stars, the images in the clouds, the mystery of seas, the transformation and renewal of all things. He was attuned to the demons of the moon who send dreams. He understood the harsh shriek of the chough, the wingsong of the swan, the resurrection of the phoenix. He could interpret the flight of crows, the course of fish, and the human voice, to predict what was to come. Legend says it was he, magician and oracle, who taught Arthur and created the Round Table. He had the respect of monsters for his knowledge and goodness and artistry, for he was a poet. He died in the Breton forest. The seed of his story was that of Lailoken, bard of Strythclyde, counsellor to the king. His lord defeated in war and killed, Lailoken lost all grip on his mind. For three days he howled and refused to eat, so great was his pain. He wailed, utterly beside himself, then fled unseen to Celidon, where he lived amid ash trees. Astonished at the sight of wild animals in the clearings, he lost his fear and joined them, eating wild plants and roots, savouring the fruits of the bushes. He became an adept of the woods.

21 August 2013
Edmonton
Concentration on a smell of ink + feckless disobedience

The Voice

the silent call of the field, the tacit offer of ripening grain, and the quiet refusal of self in the dry fallow of winter

Heidegger, "Origin of the Work of Art"

The Voice

Sometimes it is hard to tell the difference between one's voice
and one's voice

in the field or street, children are still learning
sadness from parents

one has the look of the other
immortal sadness

conducted down the river of blood
even where the cataracts spill into tremendous flicks of sunlight
and are pulverized into droplets

that land, henceforth,
on the arm
on the shoulder and on the arm

trickling to the wrist and into the hands

which makes the eye wrench upward for a single moment

2

Somewhere else, some parents are teaching "self-importance"
and the word "police"
because even the poem can be policed

and called down and despised
for feminism, for indigence,
for the word "lesbian"
which I place gently over the word "police"

because it is more peaceable

3

What other thing is there to learn from a parent

4

As such I am descended from a Mother whose own father
turned his back on war
practically deserted
because he was to be sent again into the fields of war against his brothers

and not his metaphoric brothers

his own brothers
born of the same parents

as if this desertion could make me
honest?
what new land can be ours in such circumstance

(a riposte)

And what of my Father's mother?

It is said that
the poor have nothing but the sanctity of their name

and she had inherited <portraits>

the end of the world will come with clear and unmistakable signs: children will poison their mothers in the womb with the most ingenuous of poisons (José Camilo Cela, *San Camilo, 1936*)

5

What other thing is there to learn from a parent

besides sadness
the "worthy"

what there is to teach us, they will teach us
and we will make ourselves worthy of "it"

one tree blowing in the field alone*

my own father in the stutter of time
time's gloss multipled in clocks

when time means nothing, is it revelation
or dementia
clocks, the needles of trees, the wind

(gone quiet)

(blowing in the field alone)

**to find me find the trees* (MIM)

6

Oh my brothers why are you
here where there is no river?

I am standing and my arms are
dry

I am your sister in those years forever
before our father vanished

and there is now no river just the
struts of grasses

the dry and bony rush and *kail*
of grasses

the clash and *miel* of grasses
Our parents

low <beneath> these two boot-lengths of snow

Where slatted light
Where small figures of patience
Metonymy
Selvage with an l
I was reticent before you were pyrene
I was comical before you were gay
There was a dinner party
Dad slumped in his car, sat / get up, it was time to carve
The antler-handled knives of our childhood
Treasured blades

The time comes only poetry is readable

Where slatted light
Where small figures of patience
~~Metonymy~~
(Metynomy [sic]
Salvage with an I

I was reticent before you were pyrene
I was comical before you were gay
There was a dinner party
(Dad slumped in his chair, sat up, it was time to carve
The antler-handled knives of our childhood
Treasured blades

The time comes only poetry is readable

Dementia
[and—*Allegory of Good*]

Dementia

Knowing that so-and-so wrote this
is not enough. Father, you are not my friend!
You are my father,
start being fatherly.

But you forget, you forget my friend's name,
you forget you have forgotten,
How is she doing, the one? Her name?

And on Wednesdays you won't let the nurse in,
or the doctor,
who is "trying to make a name for himself."

Forget it, Father!
It was there, it was gone, it had a name.

Let's go in circles.
It, this, the one.
The hands of the clock, yes, haunt Wednesday.
But us? We *are* us. We are still us.
A girl and two boys.
We will be there for you, we are remember.

Purpose

To draw text as one draws water from the zone
beneath the house.

To articulate all the texts of a life, as they arise.
Not separating them into poems and essays.

Creating spaces for words on pages as if they were walks or
benches.

Drinking coffee.

Drinking another coffee.
Sun on the wall. Just
sun.

Free Speech

To start, I am obliged to speak in English. Already the structure consumes me. I may write in any language I like, as long as it is Castilian or English. And so I am already speaking to you in translation, in a foreign tongue, slowly,

so I can be translated to you, all.

And I have to keep speaking in English. Because now that the simultaneous translator is assigned to me to hear my English and make Spanish (Castilian) for you, I can't empezar de falar en galego, et je ne peux parler en français non plus. Je dois modifier mes propres discours, I must modify my speaking and translate for you, in order that I may be translated.

If, as Derrida says in *Comment ne pas parler*, "The risk is inscribed in the structure," then, I would add, the banality of power is already inscribed in the monolingual structure of our exchanges today.

for María Reimóndez and Uljana Wolf

Medida

>Against the old facts and their winged jesuses
forever

Their cupboards of fabulous grain, old grain :

a grandmother's birchwood
spoon

>On the other side, fedoras or fedoræ

Custom-made Doris daybreaks

Port-passage portraits of potentates

>A generation later

Jarred moose on the basement shelves in a
bungalow

Parents who never went out dancing

Carrying a jar upstairs to her waiting mother

Ferlinghetti with grated cheese

Tr-lating Wilson Bueno

How not to speak, how to not speak, this oscillation is missing in the phrase "how to avoid speaking" that is the English title of Derrida's essay. The curious presence of the word *avoid* in this title of a talk first given in English in Jerusalem. (How the young poet waking from a coma in Montreal after the random accident, when asked: *Do you know where you are?* said: *Jerusalem.*) In English, an avoidance, whereas in French an oscillatory structure is at work: "comment ne pas – parler" exists along with "comment – ne pas parler." How can we not – *speak?* How can we *not–speak?*

Or perhaps in the English there is a nearly hidden reverberation: *how to a-void speaking?* How to unvoid it, remove its void. While trying to stay far from what will not ever stay far from us, for it adheres to us. So that we can't just ignore or abandon speech, we must *a-void* it.

In translating Wilson Bueno, there is a reverberatory relation of three languages: Portuguese, Castilian, Guaraní, across a colonial border in western Brazil.

I am creating a translation in English-with-French-and-Guaraní that perhaps no one will read.

Something unreadable, un-avoidable, un-a-voidable. And its relation to sea: a river is also the sea, infolded.

The book will "succeed" even if no one reads it. Because it will exist in the structure of English, as risk. *Paraguayan Sea.* Sea in a country with no shore but yes its rivers give unto the sea, lay claim to sea, and reach inward from sea's exteriority

inscribing the risk directly into the structure.

for Odile Cisneros and Valeria Lima

Namloz+

Questions of the sound of language, of languag&s, brisures de chocolat, the repetition of syllables in Russian, how does it transfer to English in a translated Marina Tsvetaeva poem? For it does. Rather than showing the Russian poem in Cyrillic characters opposite the English, readers of her book must open an outer ear or ear&s: on a sound file outside the space of the book, the poem is read aloud by a voice in Russian. We are here exposed to the careful plosive sense of any one word, appearing in sonic space— how can I, in writing, maintain this in the poe&s, in this poem?

Something like the drawing of the poem
treating letters as small interlocutory drawin&s

I drew them listening.

"filled with great theological light"

A small book. A workbook for heaven in and among the fires.

In the strangeness not of the wholly other but the other whole,

[approaching _ _ _ _ _]

And what of

And what of the grammar we were ~~griven~~ those years
or the one we ~~inverrnted~~
elaborate, full of beasts of the stupendous cortex
~~crawpling~~

Or were they sparrows?
Were they fearfulness with feathers, wings
not clipped but short
and the birdy parasites

Thinking about gummy things, stores of
bright light we orbited, circling
as home for these parasites
the child below us circling too

Saying "Is there a chair?" "No." "Is there a window?"
"No." Testing all of vocabulary
over and over, a parrot in small clothes
we'd buttoned him into, patient

The grammar we invented for our own vocabulary
to nourish it before we forgot
the day was that heavy

And the poem was narrative, narrative
the planet had turned and was gradually cooling
the syrup of its surface was congealing to stone
tundra, waterfalls in some places

Where the people camped and ate caribou over fires
wearing jackets,
feeling at home.

Suite aux triomphes, Frimaire XIV

When my dad flew up, his lakes were pointed in the wrong
direction.
Not like the Finger Lakes or *ooh la la* Omaha,
but streets lined up in the same immortal grid.
Calgary, hometown, under Nose Hill.
Mare Tranquillitatis.
A geographical terrain, overhead lunar, underfoot martial,
below his planes.
Do you understand the struts of anything?
You, Dad, Navigator?

Ajax, the Conqueror? A Laundry Detergent?

Suddenly gone quiet
we copy you down, Dad.
"Bring us the moon rocks, Eagle, all 47 pounds."

And the lakes? Father? Paterglyphics…

Ash trees? Melodics of old grasses.

The French habituary,
Georges Berthon, painter at Toronto, born in Vienna, *fils de René Théodore, peintre ord. de la cour de Napoléon installé à Vienne suite aux triomphes du Frimaire XIV (1805).*

The Coomlogane McCarthys. Denis espouses Lelia, *fille de Georges* (1876). Then Galicians of Toronto: F.A. Moure known as Albert weds Pauline, *soeur de Lelia* (1896). Claire, *fille de Lelia et Denis*, marries Juan, *irmán de Albert* (1911) *e pai de Merlín.*

Hello, hello. Oh hello dementia. My paternal stones.

Irish Eyes

Holes or caverns (Plato's cave with its flickers) form in the brain. Histologic findings are diffuse, with irregular loss of axons and myelin accompanied by gliosis, tissue death and altered plasticity of the arteries. The lack of neurons explains the inability to make connections, and thus the panic witnessed by grown children.

"We picked her up and I drove her out to Rideau Gardens," his brother Dick wrote of their mother's sister, Ottawa, 1954. It was the *aube* of the era of the family automobile, mark of ascension to the middle classes: when Pater Familias got in to drive, the whole family got in, aquiescent and unbelted, even if there was nowhere they needed to go.

"She's quite calm as long as we're moving, but we had to stop her from taking her dress off in the car."

Chimey Front

We chimed in and remembered.
A list of his phone numbers and their associate names was
created for him by the beautiful blond boy
(eyelashes of gold or the light from corn)

who had grown up years ago into the son.
As for him, oh *him*. He's busy. He is waiting to answer

his clock radio
and there's no phone receiver (anxious).

He is waiting in his room to receive
"shipments from the North."

Dad, Dad, Pop, Papy.
What time is it now?
What time is it, now?

How will we answer? Will you let us answer?
"No. I will answer all incoming calls."

But Papy, may we chime in?

Miming My Father

I remember him a dark dry hat in the *Chiado.*
Sparrows flew straight up an alphabet of wings
From his knees and the *praça* empty

To shadow his hat in the drawing of my father.
The funny short duck walk of a father.
Prince of steel!

Even the statue took flight out of the Lisbon square.
At its edge a closed Post Office and a burnt-in building.

I am miming my father oh cheer me on.
I am sailing out of the *Rio Tejo*
I am wearing a boat and altar—

Singing in seven generations *Pascual Bieito Juan Bill-Benito*
*Bill-Brent Troy Benjamin**

Cheer me on!
My mother's blue anorak on my back and chest
soulbright as a scapular.

Trip to Lisboa with Papai, 1994
"It was one of the best moments of my life"
**Livian Haylen Alice*

Ayam Wotayam

"It's not that I don't know who I am or what time it is [that went a long time ago, he implies], it's that I don't know what I am, or if there is an I to have an am. I wake up and think 'I must be dead.' Yet there is no 'I' thinking that. The thinking of thought, thought's thinking, is thinking 'me,' thinking *me* forward."

He gets up after that. And puts on his clothes over and over so that his body will come back into the arms of a shirt, another shirt, a jacket, two briefs, two sweaters. The sewn shares its substance with him. His substance, Bill, once neural and now vestimentary

threaded, ~~hypostatic, at~~ home.

Sentimental Poem

We're at home again on the plains of winter.
April, May, Winter.
April, and geese are still flying south.

There is something wrong with the pattern
and the wall of my heart aches
and the beams of sun.

To remember the shadow of a knife in the air
a bread knife in the kitchen
crossing my forehead. To enter its tip in the wooden door.

Wooden, Windigo, St. Orm…
Mad foot treks along the rough talus at Mt. Edith Cavell
War nurse

(whooping cough) (no strength to hunt game)

<no game>

Or your season, word?

My brother thre the nife at me, I love my brother, no one nremembers suchnoisy skriða. *Patriotism is not enough, I must have no hatred or bitterness toward anyone.* (E. Cavell, R.N.—*executed by firing squad 2 a.m. October 12, 1915. A German soldier was shot as well, for refusing to fire on her.*)

Birthday

I think I was awash in a sea of birds.
Verbs were why I wrote,

I wrote to rid myself of verbs.

Trials were alphabets, I found myself guilty, I found
myself alone
scraping letters in Edmonton on a granite stone.

I was seventeen, just barely.

I think I was awash in a dream of verbs.
Birds circled over roofs
that sheltered me.

I tried to follow you, grave verbs, all my life,
with a yellow notebook through the East of Europe
the far East of Europe, *Gad̲ Šmānê*, nearly Asia

and I am sixty-three and
I am seventeen and, dear *verbe*, next year if I am alive

I will turn twenty.

17 April 2018

Portrait of the Child E. Raising a Trout to Heaven

Tomorrow I will write the work called "human cruelty"
wherein "cruelty" and "cherish" appear
in the same strophe

and trout for that matter

a pool in the hand where fish rest shaded
and the small child lifts one up

it is so patient it lets the girl do this

for what is an image does it shimmer
in heaven where the child E. has been banished forever
her small wrists beneath the fish's fondest belly

the fish who is learning a beautiful patience
with all things

even cruelty
even with what looks like it could turn to cruelty

—heaven is dry and the Fish
in the hands of the girl is rising—

a great wind and chime are hunkered over her

Sparrow, Whiskyjack
Trout, Armistice
Crimea, Debaltseve, Altadore, the shores of Winnipeg

please don't send her away

Retrato de Pascual, Galego

Pascual Moure
Quiroga e Pardo
segundo sargento
no reximento de Monterrei
baixo o mando de Blake
Exército de Galicia
4º división
compañía primeira
na vangarda
vixiando artillería
labrego de oficio
galego enteiro
até as tripas
"campesiño mi-famento"
un deses "bandidos
dirixidos por monxes"
condecorado despois
polo seu valor e celo
nas batallas sangrentes
contra os franceses
dos exércitos de Napoleón
1808
—Medina de Rioseco
—Zornotza
—Güeñes
—Espinosa de los Monteros
todos fracasos
sen calzado en novembro
na retirada de Blake
mandados logo
para La Romana
de volta a Galicia

até as montañas súas
en farrapos e famentos
abandonados polos ingleses
Pascual Moure
segundo sargento
condecorado
escudo de distinción
1824
5 pés e 1 pulgado de altura
ollos pardos
pelo castaño claro
nariz regular
barba pechada
cicatrices de varíola
Pascual Moure
fillo de Nicolás
natural de San Clodio
esposo de Benita
—Benita Lobariñas
natural de Crecente—
retiro de inválido ás 50 anos
clase de disperso
vila de Crecente
preto do Miño
1829
18 de decembro

pai de João Benito
avó de Juan Benito
bisavó de William Benito
tataravó de Erín Claire
—que vive en Canadá
que compoñe este retrato de Pascual
que fala galego

que fala francés.

Portrait of Pascual, Galician

Pascual Moure
Quiroga e Pardo
Second Sergeant
In the Regiment of Monterrei
Under the command of Blake
Army of Galicia
4th Division
First Company
In the Advance Guard
Protecting Artillery
Labourer by Profession
Galician Fully
Right to his Organs
"Half-famished Peasant"
One of the "Brigands
Led by Monks"
Decorated Later
For Valour and Zeal
In the Bloody Battles
Against the French
Armies of Napoleon
1808
—Medina de Rioseco
—Pancorbo
—Güeñes
—Espinosa de los Monteros
All Disastrous
Shoeless in November
In the retreat of Blake
Commanded afterward
By La Romana
In retreat into Galicia

Through his own Mountains
Hungry and in Rags
Abandoned by the English
Pascual Moure
Second Sergeant
Decorated
Shield of Distinction
1824
5 feet 1 inch tall
Eyes Brown
Hair Light Brown
Regular Nose
Swarthy
Scarred by Smallpox
Pascual Moure
Son of Nicolás
Native of San Clodio
Husband of Benita
—Benita Lobariñas
native of Crecente—
Retired ill at age 50
Honourable Discharge
Town of Crecente
On the Miño River
1829
18 December

father of João Benito known as Benito
grandfather of Juan Benito known as John B.
great-grandfather of William Benito known as Bill
great-great-grandfather of Erín Claire
—who lives in Canada
who composes this portrait of Pascual
who speaks Galician

who speaks French.

“to experience what happened to speech through speech itself.” (J.D.)

Contre le prestige de la connaissance dans notre culture, il faut toujours se rappeler que la sensation et l'habitude, comme l'usage de soi, articulent une zone de non-connaissance, qui n'est pas quelque chose comme un brouillard mystique où s'égare le sujet, mais le séjour habituel dans lequel le vivant, avant toute subjectivation, est parfaitement à l'aise.

Giorgio Agamben, *L'usage des corps*, tr. J. Gayraud

cher Giorgio :
mais s'il a peur ?
la peur animal qui n'est plus—et qui est plus qu'—animal

dorénavant
coutume

Articulating the Shaking

If multilingual is to speak +one languages serially, polylingual is to speak +one languages concomitantly. It acts to induce or permit thought or affect not possible in a single and flattened linguistic realm. Did we try to dissipate what we knew or *were to know*? A "were" to knowing is a plurality, where verbs move not bidirectionally ("translation") but across multiple differential planes (*O Cidadán*), thought out polylingually

Yet we inhabit the *monolingual paradigm of translation,* in which (via German poet Uljana Wolf bringing Turkish-German Yasemin Yildiz's thinking into Musqueam/Salish Vancouver) *monolingual* means we verse one language into one other, where it confronts the *unilingual,* in which only one language exists as infinity pool or anthem with no horizon

"articulating the tunnel as shaking or cave"

Against both *mono* and *uni* lies the *polylingual*—which is *to translate an alternate memory embedded in the poems,* to quote Wolf, an embedding which thus awaits the cellular metabolism of the translator whose mitochondria are

"articulating the cave or shaking"

"paddles raised in unison }}}} standing in the boats"
}}}}

Plasticity's Foal

What we *were to know* is thus uninterpretable (for interpreters interpret from a single idiom to another singularity, obscuring the very deformations in thinking's membrane that are polylingually plastic across linguistic competencies and which make thinking thinking).

To arrive at this metabolic urgency: Namloz* (yes, Derridean, you disdreamers), the *Nameless*, those *buracos* or holes in the skull that metabolize in my dad as "a silent deterritorialization," so that "all presence," welled up, dear Papy, is "a trickle of fear."

Aphorism counter
[accidents—dementia scans—
for Pops]

preceded by
ferticule

ferticule

perhaps that
perhaps there
perhaps another where there was

a dog with its own leash in its mouth
a cat with a paw
a human with a mouth and hand

let me bow my head and reflect

perhaps that
perhaps there
perhaps another where there was

him sapiens in a blue coat
we have a word for such a blue : *bright*
vanished into the house worth $1 million

I look up from the 1941 house
grey stucco glass-dash
Fort Edmonton

ice-wall near the bones

perhaps that
perhaps there
perhaps another where there was

on this account
improvise
fir with dark birds

not frozen
scampion

merle merlot merlo
physical attraction for threes

shore advisory go home
minute lights

perhaps that
perhaps there
perhaps another where there was

snowshoes or foot toboggans
melodious snow

shy before it
melody of small bird chatter into each grain
harvest this grain
snow

edict of economy
the trace of it

"we didn't have"

subministration of water
anomaly

perhaps that
perhaps there
perhaps another where there was

here we find the setting of estranged-I

perhaps that
perhaps there
perhaps another where there was

this
reticence

spelling in schools
nineteen sixty

elefant
cirkus
miss brilz

perhaps that
perhaps there
perhaps another where there was

token of comfort
factfinder

chest open with meticulous bright saws
swans hear

clampon sivnivigance
plankton

perhaps that
perhaps there
perhaps another where there was

pulcimonious habitration
tiffalone

clapboard stucco or silk
holy monstrance

perhaps that
perhaps there
perhaps another where there was

indicate mollity
appetite serum

bólus
pahoowin
pehonan
ad <*gallaec*>
sendelle

So what?] So the ideal moment to take a picture
of the dying girl encircled by the bird of prey?
[||] Pause button
The accusation is too convenientLe situation d'exception
while the photographer is dead and the girlElle n'est pas non
plus trop d'artistesAnd their exerciseLeur accrochage muséal
[||] Pause button
Une fraction de secondeWhat is a fraction of a secondUne
seule image au-delà des stéréotypes critiquesMincing words
featuring a human being and an animalInterrupting the
accountWe know too wellEn
revanche nulle ne sait ce qu'elle est devenueIt lasts

eight minutes

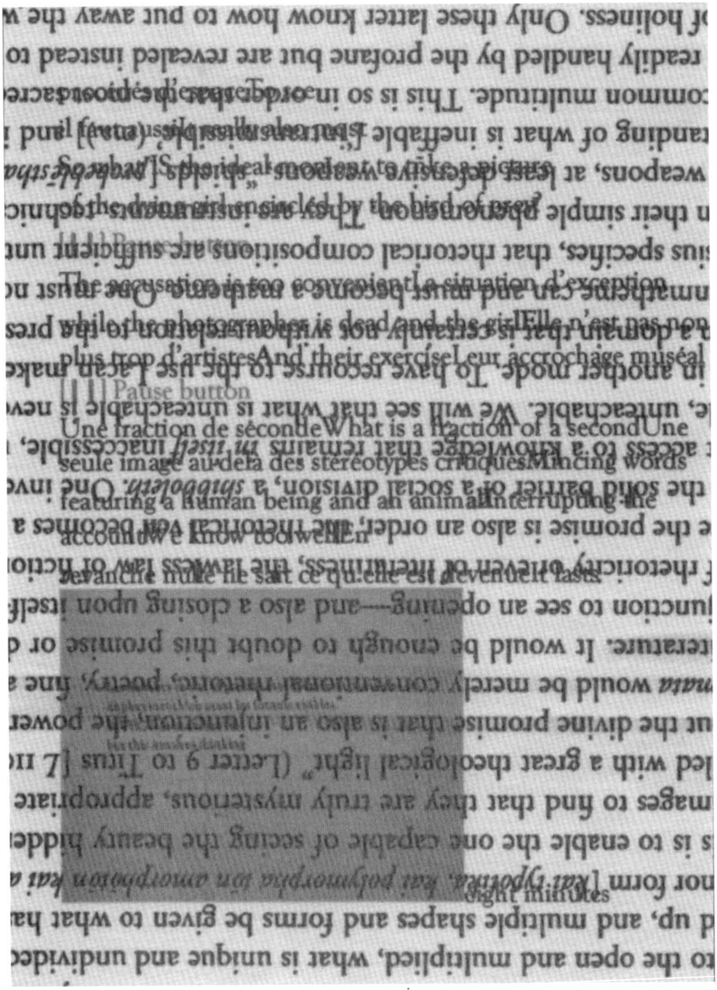

who

divine names

its ultimate failure is no less necessary. But I conc
remains at the heart of a thinking of différance or
g. It remains a question, and this is why I return to
ie same "logic," and I am still holding to the first

we will see

came from

We went to Lviv where I had a friend from school.
wanted her to finish the 6th grade of gymnasium in Lviv
a student in the medical Institute in Lviv
Ukrainians who were going to school in Lviv
Plast camp in village of Staryava, region of Lviv
in Lviv the stopover was longer
They drove me to Lviv. Scissors, penknives, and razor blades
scratched
Minsk–Gomel–Kyjev–Lviv
He lives in Lviv.
in the city of Lviv
lives in Lviv,
came from Lviv,
living in Lviv, Ukraine
Now she lives in Lviv neck always each day
He now lives in Lviv, Ukraine where he is a cantor.
From then we always lived in Lviv
I will keep my oath. Here in Lviv it is everywhere.

Created from phrases taken from witness stories at www.memoryofnations.eu which mention Lviv, sectioned by subject and each subject connected with one lock st[...]

the Glebe

teachers

"Капуста"

in words of being

or frontal spacing

one space, comma, between each line

physicality's memory,

wanting her mouth

of Arbour Lake

"You are my treasure.

"You have," she retorted, "arms."

to the syntax

limit

ries, taking in on this downward path an ever-increasing r
which multiplied with every stage of the descent. But my arg
from what is below up to the transcendent, and the more it c
language falters, and when it has passed up and beyond the as
silent completely, since it will finally be at one with him who
[*aphthenktōi*]. (*MT* 3: 1033b–c)

This economy is paradoxical. By right and in principle
movement of discourse would have negatively to re-traver
of symbolic theology and positive predication. It would th
sive with it, confined to the same quantity of discourse. In
nable, the apophatic movement cannot contain within itse
of its interruption. It c[illegible]nitely postpone the
its own limit.

Alien, heterogeneou[illegible] irreducible to the int
the experience of the [illegible] the mute vision tha
ent this apophatic, including the prayer and the praise
way—the thinking of differance would thus have little
analogous reason, with the current interpretation of cert
statements of the early Wittgenstein. I recall these word
from the *Tractatus*, for example, "6.522—The inexpressibl
[*Es gibt allerdings Unaussprechliches*]. It *shows itself*; it is the
"7.—What we cannot speak of we must pass over in silen

It is the nature of this "we must [*il faut*]" that is sig
inscribes the injunction of silence in the order or the pr

unaussprechlich

Jerusalem

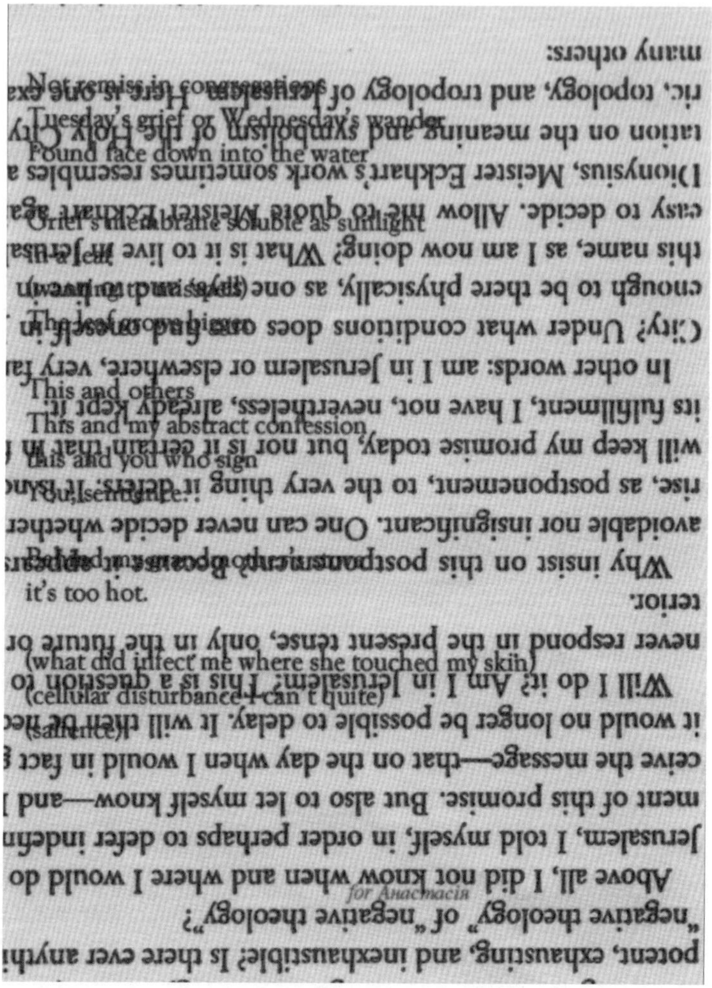

Not remiss in congregations
Tuesday's grief or Wednesday's wander
Found face down into the water
Oriel's membrane soluble as sunlight
[illegible]
The leaf [illegible]
This and others
This and my abstract confession
this and you who sign
[illegible]
[illegible]
it's too hot.
(what did infect me where she touched my skin)
(cellular disturbance I can't quite)
(salience)
for Anacmacia

cellular

a completely necessary way and as if from within—to th
ich can always become the prescriptive heading of a recon
How not to speak, what words to avoid, in order to spe
avoid speaking is thus at once or successively: how is it nece
eak? how is it necessary to speak? (here is) how it is necessa
and so on. The "how" always shelters a "why," and the "it
s the double value of a "should" or "ought" and a "must."
improvised this ~~title on the telephone~~. Letting it be dictat
not know what unconscious order—in a situation of abs
—I thus also translated ~~my desire still to~~ defer. This reactic
oduces itself on the occasion of every lecture: how to avo
d first of all how to avoid ~~committing~~ oneself by giving
ore writing one's text? But also, in the economy of the san
to speak and do it *as it ~~should be done~~* [comme il se doi
done [comme il faut], in order to assume the responsibili
e? Not only for the ~~archi-originary promise~~ that establish
responsible for speech, but for this promise in particular:
on "~~absence and negation," on the not [ne~~-*pas*] (how not t
hould not, must not, etc.), on the "how" and the "why" (
pas], the step [*le pas*], negation and denial, and so on, a
mit oneself to giving a title *~~in advance~~*. Every title has t
omise; a title given in advance is the promise of a promise.
s necessary for me to respond, but I assumed responsibili
it. Before or rather within a *double bind*: *how to avoid spea*
ve already begun to speak and have always already begun

~~rabbit~~
sprecht

(when she opened the front pocket in her mother's knapsack, out fell the *Calgary Co-op* weekly flyer.)

There was a time when M.D. lodged in the alien machines and fed waste that found in [illegible] women repeatedly accused all disasters

(its date the date of MJM's last walk in Arbour Lake— before the tumour of her brain made all motion forward in time unreal.)

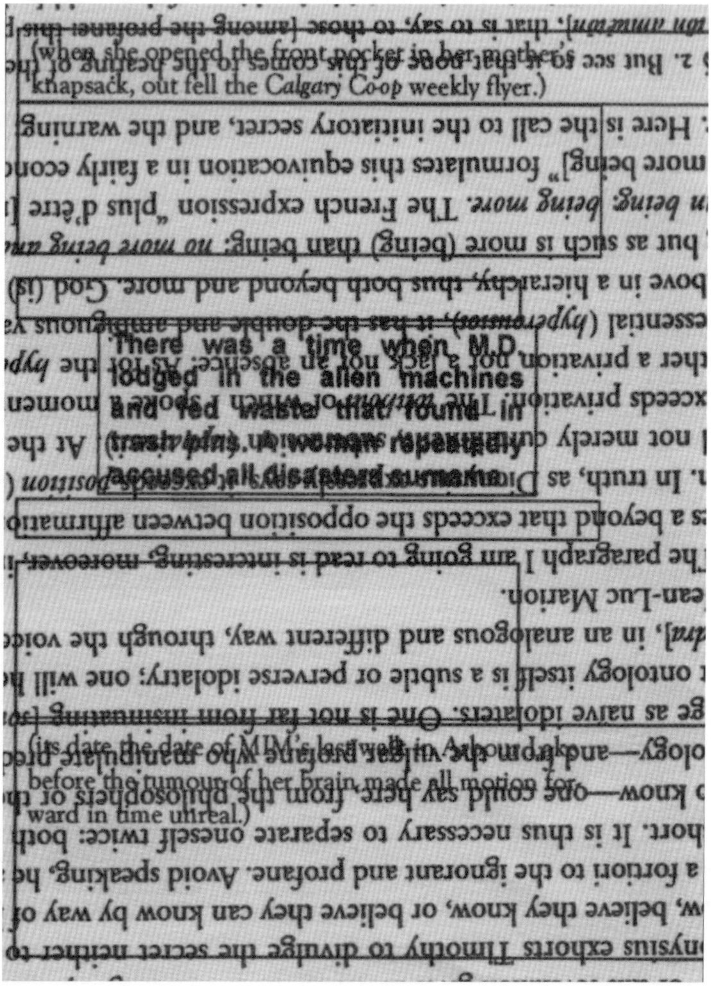

beyond and

eyes

therefore. It situates itself *beyond* all position. What is
een this place and the place of the secret, between this
the topography of the social bond that must protect
ce, there must be a certain homology. The latter must
cret—relation between the topology of what stands be-
out being [*sans être*]—without being it [*sans l'être*], and
initiatory politopology that both organizes the mysti-
nd makes possible this address to the other, this quasi-
mystagogical speech that Dionysius singularly directs to
motheon: the dedication of *The Mystical Theology*).
ny,[8] where does the speaker stand? And the one who lis-
And the one who speaks while *receiving* from the Cause
use for this community? Where do Dionysius and Tim-
they and all those who are potentially reading the text
one to the other? Where do they stand with regard to
se? God resides in a place, Dionysius says, but he is not
access to it is not yet to contemplate God. Even Moses
receives this order from a place that is not a place, even if
of God can sometimes designate place itself. Like all the
purify himself, move away from the impure, separate
many, join "the chosen priests." But access to this divine
grant him passage to the mystical Darkness where pro-
and where it is necessary to be silent. There he is finally
scribed to be silent by closing his eyes:

(a rib bone of a child rises perilously in a
bush on a hillside near Podgortzy,
Ukraine, in March 2011, frozen)
(melted snow) (March) (1943)
(the trucks came down this path)
(nauseas)
(bullet casings)
(the truck engine deaf running)

beyond

These names must speak to us; they must be written
downPeindre non la chose mais l'effet
Words are images tooAbstract neon
Donner la puissance des mots aux imagesNous forcent de
regarder leurs lettres[|||] Pause button
il ne s'agit dpas n nons priver de l'image (tort)
Thoswe who complain of the torrent are the
selectorsSournoises cette charnière-de-la
parole The images on the suucreen THEIR imagesCela veut

the holiest and highest *of the things perceived with the eye of*
mind are but the rationale which presupposes all that lies belo
dent One. Through them, however, his unimaginable prese
shown, walking the heights of those holy places [*ton hagiota*
to which the mind at least can rise. But then he [Moses] brea
away from what sees and is seen, and he plunges into the re
darkness of unknowing [*tes agnosias*]. Here, renouncing all tha
conceive ("closing his eyes" [MS]), *wrapped entirely* in the
the invisible, he belongs completely to him who is beyond ev
being neither oneself nor someone else, one is supremely u
pletely unknowing inactivity of all knowledge, and knows b
by knowing. (*MT* 1: 1000c–d; emphases added—JD)

I will take up three motifs from this passage.

1. To separate oneself, to move away, to withdraw wi
from the start this topolitology of the secret obeys an o
commanded to submit first to purification and then to dep
who have not undergone this." This order cannot be disti
a promise. It is the promise itself. The knowledge of t
who intercedes, so to speak, between God and the holy
the knowledge of the promise. Dionysius makes this clea
Ecclesiastical Hierarchy, on the subject of the prayer for t
gelia means both the commandment and the promise: "
the promises of God will surely be realized [*tas apseudeis*
in this way he teaches all those present that the gifts for

[speech—crystal—grille—

wrapped entirely

At times he spoke lucidly of the experience of dementia. You have to average all the clocks, he said. But Dad, all your clocks are wrong. If you average them, he said, you have the time of day.

Pinning time down, fairly.

In the face of terror, he developed a methodics. Torn bits of human perception he could assemble again. The *buraco* in the skull. Echo chamber

with no echoes. Bread factory. Twilight.

Then he forgot to wash, but remembered washing. He brushed only the front teeth but had brushed them all. The clothes that looked soiled to us looked clean.

His face lit up at our voices. Voices were the connective tissue to other brains with no *buracos* <His children>

credits: (how may one analyze the denial in the folds of writing—derrida) the dimension of being opens to the god who is not

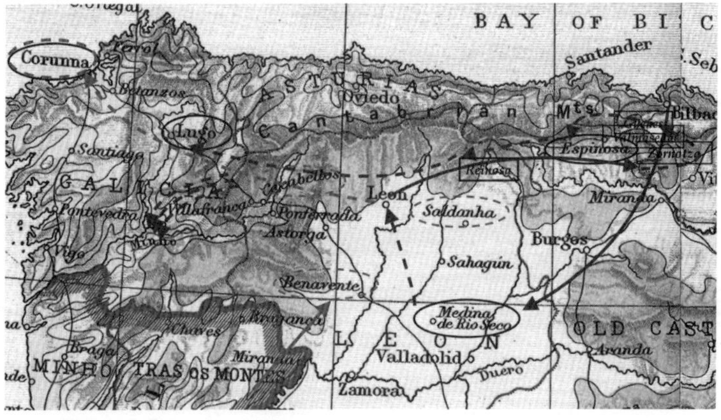

NW Spain 1808 - early 1809

broken circles: British battles

black circles: Army of Galicia battles (at Medina the Castilian Army was in charge)

broken lines: retreats

unbroken lines: advances

www.heritage-history.com/maps/philips/phil019

Torquere
[1997–]

**the space between the thing and its name, i.e. "the becoming theological of all discourse"*

Torquere

There was a sudden noise inside the person.
Her mother sent her out to buy a carton of "Craven As."
There was an explosive ticking inside the person.
We didn't have a French accent.
She wore notoriety's explicit conveyance:
A loud voice.
All the alcohol and no drinking.
Taking up horticulture with a hoe.
She shaved 2 minutes off the word "light."

There was a gradual infinitum.
All this description is as false as language.
Do you see exactly?
Our imperative?
Why not commemorate these other frays.
Why not exacerbate momentum.
All the children wore signs of terrible used Ritalin.
We know them before their name.
There was a sudden cracking blow inside the person.
Y avait un craquement soudain à l'intérieur de la personne.

A tree lost its first limb, crushing her red car.
After that she obeyed baking.
Corpuscles were found scattered over the asphalt, their loud devices.
Fortitude's leaf bloomed.

There was a resounding noise inside the person.
Y avait un bruit retentissant à l'intérieur de la personne.
Saliva metabolized the RNA of milk cows and flies.
Drinking produced another incident, then
later a sick tum.
There was a terrible clicking noise inside the person.
The substance produced as a by-product of embroidery
Turned out to be toxic.
(A) touched (B)'s breast, struggling
Around the pronoun difficulty.
The coast was clear. They got up.
(B) watched the worn spot on (A)'s jeans.
There was a harsh careen inside the person.
The message was brought forward into
"Today's Business."
Even someone with 3 times her capacity would not have made it
After all.
She made up an excuse and returned home,
Not wanting to get in a tizzy.

Genetic insouciance prevailed, an Olds Cutlass.
Divisions were consonants, then repeated.
Her rogue hand opened X to insert a finger.
There was a hard thwack inside the person.
Y avait une gifle dure à l'intérieur de la personne.
The bacterial fracture guides us.
Her axon imprint staged life amid "lavoir."*
Obelisk manifest
Arrayed.

**tolle lege*

There was a scorching crash inside the person.
Y avait un choc brûlant à l'intérieur de l'être de la personne.

Trees wilted or witnessed (no one heard).
Particulate erupt.
Her side of the bed emptied out of lust,
Which caused the other (B) anguish.
There was a mordant wail inside the person.
Il y avait un cri perçant à l'intérieur de la personne.
There was a worsening error inside the person.
A huge crash stopped the traffic of the corpuscles (B).
A huge crash stopped the traffic inside the skin (B).
The sun burned down on their heads in the crashed vehible.
A huge crash halted corpuscles rictus endogamy (B).
A huge crash mortar thrown epinephrine abend (B).
A huge crash homily heartstroke incipient tracheotomy
//}»

wick winter wrung wrestled wreckible wren
//}»

(B).

En péril

Le territoire m'a abattu
Quel territoire

Sonne à ma porte je te le dirai
je te le montrerai (mon veston de miséricordes)

L'avenir est venu dans un seul mot
territoire (ce mot-là)

avec qui

2

Au cas où
« obligatoire »
une phrase méchante de mon vocabulaire

ou de ma maladie
cachée à l'avant
du cerveau

troupeaux
vêtements déchirés
quelle mode   (de vie)

coupable ou

avec quoi

3

Les réligieuses en mitaines sont amusantes aujourd'hui
veux-tu bien que je te raconte *cela*?

« un mouchoir échappé au jardin »

ridicule
ce n'est pas racontable

après toute cette déception
L'infini

je m'excuse, je me trompe
je suis (coma sempre) trop bornée par des rêves

En perigo

Abateume o territorio
Que territorio

Toca á miña porta e vouche dicir
vou amosarche (a miña chaqueta de misericordias)

Chegou o futuro nunha soa palabra
territorio (que palabra)

con quen

2

No caso
"obrigatorio"
unhas palabras desagradábeis do meu vocabulario

ou da miña enfermidade
ocultada na fronte
do cerebro

rabaños
roupa resgada
que modo (de vida)

culpábel ou

con que

3

As monxas en luvas están tan divertidas hoxe
queres que che conto isto?

“pano de papel caído no xardín”

ridículo
xa non é contábel

despois de toda esa decepción
O infinito

desculpe, estou equivocada
c’est que je suis trop confinée par mes rêves

Vestimentary

It was my father's own mother
wrote his eldest brother, gayly
of his first leave home from basic training, Xmas 1940

Will you wear your Uniform?

All his life my father kept his brother Harry's letters
written from the Royal Ottawa San

Never showed any of us

2

Uncle Harry
TB
Camp 31 Cornwall Ontario
veteran whose only war took apart his lungs
rib after rib
letter after letter
leaving striped pyjamas in a sanatorium, 1952
and inked messages of prayer

3

Dad
Air Force veteran
gripping the seam of bedsheet, oxygen monitor pacing
his finger red
see-sawing his thin arm through engine failure

holding steady in havoc
                                        through storm cloud

"look out—
don't touch that—we're going down!"

4

Me
Daughter
in the trees amid a *tremble* of leaf-light (aspen, birches)
blue anorak over my shoulders
I am my mother's daughter watching, 2013
Merlín

vanquish
fin all y
his ever y [sidestep]
                                    war

IN OTHER words, language estranges the human and we let it utter us. The pre-eminent means of taking the measure of the distance that separates a body from the sky is, to Hölderlin, poetry. All Galicia in insurrection, Soult's weary French left for Portugal, desperately seeking shoes, food, and rest for men and horses. East of Ribadavia, as the invaders marched on their way to Ourense to cross the Lethe on the *ponte romana* and head south through the Limia, the monks again emerged from the woods to pretend peace. The feeling of existing that arises from the mouth is anterior to any form of self-consciousness. Even the blood of the body is perceived as belonging to the earth. But if every act of thinking is a problem, how is "becoming" possible? At dawn, amid strewn bodies of attackers felled in the pitch of night by their line troops, light infantry, and dismounted dragoons, the French found the very monks who had promised peace, mouths opened to the sky, lips black from tearing cartridges.

19 February 1809
Ribadavia

we raise our hands not in supplication but in revolt

Absence from History
[Intesta e.]

What Gone Is (1)

Gone is the inner connective light. The
mark of words or words between words goes
missing, admonished. Or still. The grass
blades grow upward. Or obvious. I who can
take joy in anything, feel joy, learn joy from
the last lap around the block or desert, the
feeling of inner light is gone,

passably

the passably urgent.

(In the dream we are a band called Noise Vulvas. Two girls and a boy. My friends say that when I say boy I mean man but I mean boy. In the band we give ourselves names like Ketchup Sunday, then laugh and name ourselves back again. In Spain I am embarassed by my whole name, only *Moure* sounds real, sounds solemn. All the rest could be vulva noise.)

The mark of the scars sealing over inside the
body, where the cuts were made. A map of these
cuts.

(A boy runs up, holding a huge lamprey against
the stone. Its face echoes open river water, now
running upward toward us.)

(socket wrench)

belief

keep the generations separate (the cold depth)
the letters (imagined) keep them as imagined
socket [0:33][0:54][1:56][2:19][4:52][5:10]

the layers of this remembered world, this chaos and unmentionability in her mother's family (no one gained) but we can't forget who it was <Jews> who suffered annihilation

arc and movement onstage of the chairs

Cold Depth (2)

The tapping of the incision later by the
physician's hands moving down the layers
of the abdominal wall. A gate or door to the
interior;

(Where the boys caught the lamprey, a cold
depth. In one sense, Ourense; in the other,
the sea. Huge sucking mouth of the fish or
tube they lifted it up the hill, others in front
of them heralding the way, shouting. Above,
stands of eucalyptus light. Register.
Crecente. Meu Lar.)

(there are people who are terribly lonely)

"go out and enjoy the day"

(It is not her father's fault and not her brother's fault just something she doesn't understand What she doesn't understand is absence What she doesn't understand is presence but she knows the power of memory to make anything present The wind inside the head that can pick up whole rivers and smash them against the road The wind inside a shell the sound of the sea People have leapt asunder hearing this sea)

There are people who are terribly light who
hear the wind inside themselves

Riches count for more than anything else

in America

[0:33] at death of mother <banquets>
[0:54] instructions for reading <Calgary>
[1:56] can't distinguish
[2:19] and here would be a chance for siting
[4:52] "I wanted to marry you"
[5:10] pyrogy
[torch]
[6:32] there is a gentleness and passivity in these words "it was made of wood"

The Choreograph (3)

The track of the incision; ciphers red on the
abdomen. Clamp marks gradually imbibed
by the body, leaving a tide line.

(The girl looks at me. "Sorry" she says, a
word she knows as a word of courtesy,
though she means "hello." She has been
down at the river, drinking a dark pool
under the eucalyptus by the *serradoiro*.)

(a healing matter)

socket [0:33][0:54][1:56][2:19][4:52][5:10]

(A lot of taboos have already been broken. Fierce dogma sings out, win this tune. A woman in a fur hat singing absalom absalom. Advisory for someone smoking a bit. An entire systole has been written under this hat. A table burnished for all we know. Knowing is falling or, fainting backward.)

It appeareth simply as light. A place in the
chest wherefrom spring vocables. Or the old
words "in street clothes," the backdrop of.
The mark of words is missing, this we speak
of. Impassive in the face of, a stone light

Worldl>-·

the choreograph;

knowable

Effects   Orphects   Infects   Confects

operates and flips

verticality emerges: the possibility of hierarchy in the book
and how she (Brossard) turns that, laterally across the line itself

(writing on the ethics of an intervention)

cortical light (dopplegänger of water)

dear nicole
dear fred
dear amy

(at work at dawn) (Costco® across the river)
[torch][6:32]

Relief (4)

Is it an escape world to go to in the head Is
it heaven Is it the hell of the personal Or
corruption of friendship that thing we were
sure existed I mean woman not girl Is it just
inner pain

passably

the contingent; [2:19][4:52]

(In my dream her face rises as she stands in the fields nearby bulls
with their yellow ear tags and soft faces crying love the loam
flecked on their legs. A green shirt. Sky slate grey about to rain.)

The field or page of my abdomen or chest,
where the cuts were made. A map on a body
of these cuts.

(A boy runs up against the yellow grass.
Later he will become a eucalyptus cutter in
the groves of Sendelle, holding history in
his head the names for things those bisected
names Xoán, Joán, Juan, John, Bieito,
Benedict, Benito, Ben)

(the great saw extended)

relief

(he emigrated) (the girl remained) (the son) (the grandchild)

(South Peace)

→

S a s k a t o o n   M o u n t a i n

(cut here)..................[the space of artifice]..........................

(fold here).................. [the space between parents] ....

(Fentiman Avenue)

map of
Ottawa

F:-/old

Willow

Wind, the creak of boughs—telegraphy. This evening—stark
Happiness. Bits of Laughter stuck in the trees. No one had eaten all
the food—not plausible. Coffee, potatoes, wine's hormone ensues
in human thought. We adopted la langue française (my brother
and I). And loved cursive writing. It's very handy, in particular.
Because of the corporeal relation, thoughts can be recorded in fact
very quickly if you hold the pen in a light grip. And ballpoint ink
recalls antique perfumes. My first time buying one in Calgary—age
seven, Altadore Drugs on 16th, 10¢—I walked north past Jake &
Jim's the Mormon barbers, the pen cupped to my mouth and nose.
Tremendously wanting to write and to be alongside thinking.
To draw on the text as one draws water from a zone beneath the
house.

Concentration on a smell of ink + feckless disobedience
Invisible sovereignty of gesture
My dad, who lost all except his gestures (yes he gave me that 10¢

Wind.
Telegraphy.
An elevator.
A plane.
An elderly man at the controls, his thumb lit red (O_2 saturation)

Dear Father. Or willow. For truth is that it grows aslant the brook (act 4, scene 7, H-t.) *as if to tell: below us all, where willow roots seek loam and clay, there is ever running water. Love, a daughter.*

Shiny Front

Is it you, sadness? Maudite tristesse
qui chiffre ma tête si jeune
Chiffrée

picotée
de graines, de la raison
en graines

Aujourd'hui,
pas mieux

Is that you, wayside station?
School-patrol badge polished up with spit?

Overcoat with the shiny front?
Running shoe with fresh hole?

Winter's coming...

Static ahem?

we all ran out of the house when he was angry, but the house is demolished now.

Measure for a Long Wound (Wednesday was such a bad day)

I am thinking of thinking and unthinking under the
currently thought
circumstances of thinking

I got up at 2:30 a.m. to read Frank O'Hara
I took 2 aspirins for headache (we were falling off the porch
laughing last night)
Whom I believe in

There are ambiguities in this life that are, as Ken would say
"entirely" beautiful

Wanting only to be adept at what I do, I compress all of it
even time
Trying to get words out of the head fast as possible before they
vanish
The lake rises under the storm, I don't mean any lake, I mean this
lake
"Lake Hmi-hmoo"
Swollen water pouring over a lifted bed of stone
It's weak stone anyhow, it's old seashore, it crumbles

We can only lie down in the tents of our minds
Our chests upward breathing and legs touching the sheet cotton
two legs, whole
The fans moaning, stir the heat up
We humans, it was us
invented sunbathing and the word "strafe" the words "civilian
population" the word "person"
Animals look at us dumbfounded aren't we all the same

Roar

At stall speed this shut world terrifies
A wall goes up in frames

Physically uncertain at the distal midgins of the rody

Ache Tuesday
Ache Wednesday
Thursday up for breakfast waited an hour for coffee
by that dining room clock its needles always wrong

Yes it is me who called "Bullshit" in the dining room
out loud

The waiter reported me, I am called on the carpottete

The manager of old beings said I swore
I said I spoke no name of any god

I said I spoke a common barnyard syllable
Yes it was out loud

And dammit I waited too long for my coffee
A client should be treated better

not taken into custody on this very carpottete

And I stand by my roar

signed Bill

Riverbend Retirement Living by Revera®, Edmonton AB

It could be a story of translation and the light of the poem, or it could be a stubborn ongoingness despite missing gills, or the dark matter of the universe we can only know when it refracts off the gravity of light bodies, as if the wooing of the beloved is the act that sustains a world, breathes a materiality of fish or fuel...

and the a-void of language in us as sp-eaking

the "how to" "not–speak" and its de-negation

my dad as in Pasolini's film on Matthew where Filippo, not-yet apostolic, glances sidelong without a word, yet from his eyes we know him as subject to interpellation (before he knew)

what is rigour here, what abstinence, what fortitude

and pull the ladder up

"shot without wound"

“I was flooded with relief”

Art’s freedom to move
Without falling into solipsism
Art arises from life
Without falling into imitating ideologies we agree with

Question:

How to maintain that tension as productive
« agent pour une possible guérison », kenneth tynan
in ionesco’s *notes et contre-notes* (Folio) 147
150 orson welles « la moindre parole que profère un artiste est l’expression d’une attitude sociale »

Reread also:
158
Arguing for the constructivity of the superfluous
on a stage where life

(arises from art*

I am not capitulating.
Bérenger’s last sentence, Rhinoceros, *Eugene Ionesco (1959)*

The struggles of thinking our book, dear Dad. Wherefore I have your papers; in them, your obsession with accounts and laundry, no voices. The invasions of Napoleon (a thick file). Joyful letters handwritten then typed into emails. Yet I remember conversations:

"I woke up and Billy was sitting in the chair at the end of the bed"

"I don't think so, Dad"

"He was sitting there"

"Then where is the chair?"

(...)

"Dad?"

(...)

"Possibly you were dreaming."

"I don't believe I dreamed."

"Where did the chair go?"

"He took it with him!"

"How did he get in?"

"Someone gave him a key."

— —

Old letter found from Dad to Dadself, dated and timed like a flight log, upon getting up the courage to phone MIM, still alive; unable to believe in the permanence of separation

who are you, Billy Mouré, Billy Shushkeebob, Billy Shy Grin?

"We had a conversation for 15 minutes. A new start?"

Хромотопа

The word "GALEGO" flashes

The window, the tree, the French-speaking policeman

A torn bit of the Irish prisoner's shirt

A facial prosthesis for a wounded Guernsey cow

Fount frontal of poo

Two false sapiens snicker

A coffin for the Magus, with a hole to let piss out the other side

Jeopardy in yellow skirts

Restless leg syndrome

A war airport given back to nesting skylarks

Berlin airlift in girlish memory

Where chromotopes —time's colours— are at home

One year before

March 29, 2012
Dear Erín! Wow, here I am back in my room
By coincidence, last night I was enjoying a reread of the book about Daisy Callison, whose trek

March 11
I find it difficult to make plans because of changeable weather and because I need to spend time at Riverbend and get caught up on my paperwork. And think about new clothes: sports jacket needs replacement.
NB Tell Ken about lamp that keeps falling over.

Saturday March 10, 2012. Reset clocks. Spring FWD.

Apr 01 Ricardo started up my TV machine. But I am still having difficulty to turn TV on or off!

Mon. morning. It appears like some tax payments may be due (check w. Bill!)
Correct time as shown on wall clock.

Regular business envelope or greeting card: use one P stamp.
For same weight in large env. (use 2 P stamps)

Three months before

I have no boats!

A Walk on Jasper Avenue After the Death of My Father

Sometimes on the street on the face of a stranger, I see the mouth of my father.
Father who is not my father!
Sleep of Dad!

Child who is not even child of himself!
Child who is child of his old mother, not mine but his, or not even his,
not anyone's.

Child who is Orphan here! Aching for happiness.
Smiles… hand… leaves… tree…
Skein of life… hand… leaves… tree…. orphic…

Mouth of Dad, why are you speaking?

Mouth of my father voyaging down an avenue on the face of another…

Solace… you are alive!

Sleep, why did you call me…

You woke me…

Oh sleep now, mouth of my father, sleep in the air of a hallway, a ward in the Royal Alex where you'd first met our mother, arrived on a bus from the air base, in the blue serge of a Navigator of Canada, now wartime is over, may the Allegory of Good watch over your dreamings, hush and find sleep now, steady in storm cloud, oh Dad, oh Papai, we're with you, when the red light on the rudder of oxygen stops blinking, we're with you forever, Erín Ken Billy, there's nothing to fear

Homage the power of potato
transl. William Benito Moure

the potato found in ~~an~~ a mixture   very savage
of the water and flame
within the earth.
and a mixture (very) concentrated no planet
same net made of powder not able to mix
water and flame.

- -

for ese? a power revolutionary the potatoes
and then the powder
in effect
to/for? increase the power to powder, precise?

...magnolias.
when speech somebody the powder and magnolias
an implicit message of the potential of potatoes

water and flame
fire water solid

sea without ________

shot without wound

February 13, 2003
my dad learning Galician backwards
by translating from *Little Theatres*
found 2017 and copied by EM

ACKNOWLEDGEMENTS

Brazil: Zunái; *Galicia:* As Escollas Electivas, Canada & Beyond; *Switzerland:* Dusie; *USA:* Harper's, Connotation, Gulf Coast Review, *Resist Much Obey Little,* ed. Kent Johnson & Michael Boughn; *Canada:* Event, Herstory 2015, Rampike, Hazlitt, newpoetry.ca, The Walrus, Touch the Donkey, The Apostles Review, Vallum, Poetry Gabriola. *Aphorism Counter* was a 2018 Elephant Book, thanks to Jordan Scott & Broc Russell. *Absence from History* was a live performance with composer Lee Hutzulak, commissioned by Poetry Gabriola. Huge thanks to Green College at UBC for the 2015 residency that let me work. Thanks to Oana Avasilichioaei for crucial first edits, Lisa Robertson for pushing me hard at the end. Thanks to my dad, who wanted to write this book with me in Edmonton and who sends readers his regrets; his passion for the Peninsular War and modernity became mine. For sustenance: Ken, Bill, Kim Fullerton, Lou Nelson, Emeren García, Belén Martín Lucas, Chus Pato, Chantal Neveu, Oana, Lisa, and Karis Shearer.

1) The "dementia scans" were decided by a printer that crashed pagescapes from Derrida's "How to Avoid Speaking: Denial" beneath poems from *The Unmemntioable.* In them, I recognize my dad's mind: not citation, but picture. 2) Duns Scotus's *haecceity* or "thisness" was fished back to Aristotle's *to ti esti* (τὸ τί ἐστι), "the what (it) is": the invisible sovereignty of gesture. 3) In the decades of Franco repression, Arthurian legend often buoyed Galician literature (Cunqueiro, Ferrín) when political struggle & Galician difference could not be spoken, thus Merlín (an unspeakable beauty that endures). 4) "Verbatio" is Duns Scotus: *Et hoc quia 'verbatio' quod est abstractum huius concreti 'verbum' videtur illam relationem primo significare per respectum ad verbantem* (Reportatio Examinata 1A). To wit: "Wording," the abstract noun that corresponds to the concrete "word," mainly signifies via a relation to the one who speaks.

Www.youtube.com/watch?v=_innxt6Oesw. Dark Elderberry Branch: Poems of Marina Tsvetaeva *I. Kaminsky & J. Valentine.* (NY, 2012). Mémoires sur les opérations militaires des Français en Galice, en Portugal, et dans la Vallée du Tage en 1809 sous le commandement du Maréchal Soult, Duc de Dalmatie *P. M. LeNoble, chevalier* (Paris, 1821); History of the War in the Peninsula and in the South of France from 1807 - 1814 *William F. P. Napier* (London, 1828).

Envoi:

> ***In the absence of poetic* razón*:***
> ***To make wording for my father,***
> ***To retrace my own meridian.***

WHERE LIFE coincides with its form, to have life is to live. A descendant of the abbott whose monks and *labreg@s* had laid seige to Mourentán bridge in 1809 to defend his privilege claimed in the deposition (Creciente, 16 Dec^{r}, 1881) to be an intimate friend of the deceased Juan Benito, emigrated son of La Romana's sergeant Pascual, and demanded power of attorney to sell the estate (a leira of vines, a hib, a copper boiler for distilling *augardente*) on behalf of the widow Moure now settled in Toronto near her own brother who would help her. Such was the freedom for which the insurgents of Galicia fought bitterly: emigration of their children to Paris, to London, to the Humber River, their inheritance plundered, impunity of the police and the division of the human body, arduous in the field of sky, for Being itself, as we read in Heidegger, is always and obstinately delivered up to something inassumable and obscure, held in suspense, illuminating its very core, keeping open the question of "Who?" and guarding the concealed in self-conce&lment, thus in translation there can be no loss as each text constitutes its subject, rowing a small *verbatio'*

a history that has had no place in poetry
a name Troncoso that cannot be mentioned
an explanation without an ear now & forever

i raise my hands with yours not in supplication but in revolt
}}}} }}}}